GLASGOW
BLUE TRAINS
CLASS 303 AND CLASS 311 EMUs

COLIN J. HOWAT

AMBERLEY

First published 2023

Amberley Publishing
The Hill, Stroud
Gloucestershire, GL5 4EP

www.amberley-books.com

Copyright © Colin J. Howat, 2023

The right of Colin J. Howat to be identified as
the Author of this work has been asserted in
accordance with the Copyrights, Designs and
Patents Act 1988.

ISBN 978 1 3981 0568 3 (print)
ISBN 978 1 3981 0569 0 (ebook)

British Library Cataloguing in Publication Data.
A catalogue record for this book is available from
the British Library.

Origination by Amberley Publishing.
Printed in the UK.

Introduction

November 1960 was a major day in the history of the Glasgow rail system as it was when the first of the new electric Blue Trains entered service on the suburban routes, thereby replacing the old steam locomotives from all tunnel routes below the city. These three-car units did not get off to a great start. They were soon all taken out of service due to serious failures and it was many months before the city of Glasgow would see the full electric service. The Blue Trains, classified officially as AM3 and AM11, later Class 303 and 311, were once the backbone of electrified services in the Glasgow area. That is until route expansion saw newer forms of traction delivered from the late 1970s and late 1980s, with the Class 314, 318 and 320s starting to enter service. Based on the Mk 1 bodyshell design, the Class 303 units utilised electrical gear made by Metropolitan-Vickers. A few years later, further expansion of the Glasgow electrified network saw the 303 and 311 units going further away, mainly within the Strathclyde area although some reached Edinburgh for driver training in connection with the North Berwick line from 1989. In fact, they were ultimately replaced on this line, as BR stated that three cars were unsuitable. They were replaced by the four-car 305 units from the Eastern Region.

Electrification in Glasgow started with the energisation of the Glasgow Queen Street Low Level lines connecting Airdrie, Springburn and Bridgeton Central in the east with Helensburgh Central, Milngavie and Balloch Pier to the west. The official launch was accompanied with an elaborate publicity campaign. Stations along the route were adorned with the new symbols of the electrification scheme – the blue and yellow arrow intertwined into a helix shape – hanging high up outside most stations. Posters and publicity literature featured the slogan 'Best Travel Blue Train'. It worked wonders. Within weeks, the passenger journeys on the north side had leapt to 400,000 a week – over three times the figures of the old steam-powered services. The electrified lines were energised using the overhead power system, which in the city generally used 6.25 kv and in outer areas the full 25 kv ac supply. The lower 6.25 kv system was introduced in areas of limited clearance between bridges and areas of limited head room due to the magnetic induction caused by the full 25 kv. Technological advances by the late 1970s allowed these areas to be also converted to the full 25 kv systems. The south side of Glasgow followed a similar pattern and from 1962 the lines from Glasgow Central High Level to Neilston and Motherwell via the Cathcart Circle were also electrified. The north and south side systems operated as separate electrified railways until the Argyle Line was opened up in 1979. This allowed stock to move between Hyndland Depot in the north to Shields Depot in the south without the need for the units to be hauled by diesel.

Rolling stock for both the north and south side consisted of a fleet of ninety-one Class AM3s (303s) built between 1959 and 1960 at the Pressed Steel Factory at Linwood, near Paisley. A further batch of AM11 (311s) were ordered from the same company when electrification was extended from Glasgow to Gourock and Wemyss Bay in 1967, which amounted to an additional nineteen units. The original order for the 303s was for thirty-five, but it was soon realised that this would have to be increased, and ninety-one in total were actually constructed.

Each three-car 303 was formed of two driving trailers and an intermediate motor coach, giving a formation of Driving Trailer Standard Open (DTSO), Motor Brake Standard Open (MBSO) and a Battery Driving Trailer Open (BDTSO). The MBSO housed all the electrical and traction equipment. It also housed the guard van and, on the roof, the power-collecting pantograph. Traction equipment was supplied by AE1 Metropolitan Vickers and included a mercury arc rectifier and four 207 hp (154 kw) traction motors. The units were fitted with electro-pneumatic-controlled air brakes and had a top speed of 75 mph (121 km/h). The units had many features, which made them state of the art at the time of their introduction. This included the use of pneumatically operated sliding passenger doors (the only Mk 1-based EMU to use this feature), with passenger-operated, door-opening buttons. In practice, the doors were usually operated by the train guard (later driver, after modification for driver-only operation).

Units were semi-permanently coupled, permitting interchange of vehicles if required. This did happen on occasions, particularly in the late 1970s when the transition from BR standard blue to BR blue and grey liveries took place. A full-width driving cab was provided at both ends of the DTSO coaches, with the driving position on the left side. End connections consisted of a buck-eye coupler and pullman rubbing plate, body-mounted air connections and a multiple-control jumper cable and socket. A cant rail height destination indicator was provided, and a two position route indicator was carried on the front end below the middle window. Glass partitions behind the cabs allowed passengers in the front and rear most carriages to see the drivers view of the track. This was particularly appreciated on the scenic riverside areas around Gourock and Helensburgh. Originally the driving and non-driving side front windows were curved onto the bodyside, but from 1972 these were replaced gradually with flat, strengthened, glazed windows following an accident when a driver was struck by an object thrown at his train that penetrated the curved screen and killed him. Each unit was originally made up for a total of 236 standard-class passengers on comfortable, deep-sprung seats set out in a 2+3 high-density styling. Passengers sitting at the front of a unit had the added benefit of a forward view the same as the driver, as long as the light blind was left up.

Originally, the units were presented in an attractive Caledonian blue livery with a thin yellow band below the windows – hence the units were originally known as the 'Glasgow Blue Trains'. Unit Nos 303001–056 operated on the north side while Nos 303057–091 worked on the south side. The fleet was soon operated as a common pool. However, the north and south sides were not connected physically until the Argyle Line was reopened in 1979. In later years it was also possible to run from Yoker Yard to Shields Depot via Whifflet when the single line between Sunnyside Junction west of Coatbridge Sunnyside and Whifflet was electrified. This used the overhead equipment removed from the Balloch Pier stub. The Lanark to Milngavie services were diverted over this line when the Argyle Line was closed due to flooding in 1995 and in 2022 when the Argyle Line was again closed for refurbishment. As the Class 303s were air-braked and as most diesel locomotives of the early era were vacuum-braked, a few Class 20 diesels were fitted with air brake connections for any depot moves. Although, when the Class 303s were new there were still a few former Caledonian Railway 4-4-0 steam locomotives in stock with Westinghouse air brakes, which were used for the transfers and also for delivering the units from their factory at Linwood.

From their introduction, two depots were responsible for the 303 maintenance. On the north side this was Hyndland Depot and on the south side it was Shields Depot. Originally the 303s were serviced and had major work carried out at Hyndland Depot, which was built specifically for the 303 fleet. Later on, major work was transferred to Shields Depot, which had been expanded in 1967 to cater for the additional 311 units for the new electric services to the Inverclyde area. These further nineteen near-identical units released in 1967 were built by Cravens in Sheffield. Hyndland depot eventually closed in 1987 when all maintenance was concentrated to Shields Depot.

On Saturday 5 November 1960, 303s were introduced into passenger service. Trains were well liked by passengers and staff, with hundreds of people flocking to sample the new services. A good benefit of the new units was the cleaner atmosphere; previously, steam trains working through Glasgow city centre tunnels were a major health hazard. Journey times were vastly reduced with faster acceleration, higher speeds and improved braking. Soon after the introduction of the new services major problems and failures in electrical systems were found, including burnt-out motor windings. The following day, Sunday 6 November, unit 021 was found to have smoke emitting from its transformer. Three days later unit 014 had a major transformer issue. These incidents, together with others, resulted in the entire fleet being taken out of traffic for further inspections and action.

The MBSO vehicles from the first batch of fifty units had to be stripped and rebuilt, while those still under assembly were upgraded on the production line. Due to the withdrawal of the 303s, steam traction with old suburban stock had to be hastily reintroduced onto all Glasgow electrified routes. This will all mean that at the time and the Scottish Region pulled off a remarkable interim emergency timetable.

Upgrading and repairs for the 303s took a long time to complete and it was not until 1 October 1961 that the units returned to passenger service. On 27 May 1962, the south side electrification was opened up, with services now running from Glasgow Central to Neilston, Cathcart Circles and Motherwell via Newton. In the mid-1960s a number of modifications continued to be made to the fleet. This included strengthening of vestibule floors and door upgrades. In conjunction with this unit 035 was fitted with 'plug doors', which opened outwards and slid along the outside of the coach body. The same unit was later subject to further development testing in 1967 when thyristor control equipment was fitted. Another major traction trial involved unit 071, which was fitted with silicon rectifiers in place of the previous mercury rectifiers. Eventually this equipment was fitted to the rest of the fleets.

The 311s were very similar to the 303s, but the 1967 build had extra air grilles on the MBSO body, and from their introduction they were fitted with fluorescent lighting. The interiors of the Class 303s had been fitted with tungsten light bulbs. The 311s were also fitted with more powerful traction motors of 890 hp (660 kw). These units were delivered and painted in standard BR rail blue. The West Coast electrification in 1974 saw the Lanark branch and Hamilton Circle lines both electrified, and so the 303 and 311s were deployed to these areas as well. The joining of the north and south electric areas took place in May 1979 when the Argyle Line was reopened, connecting both sides of the River Clyde. Driver training began quickly, with Yoker and Motherwell drivers leading up to the eventual official reopening of the line by Elizabeth II later in the year, in November. This also saw the introduction of the new Class 314 units, which were to work alongside the 303 and 311 units.

During 1981, due to a combination of a fall in passenger numbers, rationalisation of services and better use of units, twelve 303 units were transferred to the London Midland region and based at Crewe and later Manchester Longsight for use on various routes in and out of Manchester Piccadilly. These were unit Nos 303036/041/045/050/053/059/060/066/067/078/082. No 311 units were transferred. Most of these units were repainted into the Greater Manchester PTE orange and brown livery. Initially, they were used on the Crewe to Liverpool service, but were soon transferred to other routes, including Altrincham, Hazel Grove, Macclesfield, Alderley Edge and Hadfield. All but one of these, No. 303048, were withdrawn by the mid-1990s. This unit was then transferred back north to Shields Depot in Glasgow and retained in unrefurbished condition for special trains. It was also painted in Caledonian blue livery. It was originally intended to preserve this unit, but due to asbestos contamination it was eventually scrapped in 1996. It was later replaced in preservation by a combination of coaches from units 023 and 032.

The Class 303s started to be withdrawn from use in Scotland in December 1982 when a handful of units were sidelined. The following year, with the era of rail blue and grey starting to go, the first application of Strathclyde orange and black began to appear for the first time. The first unit to be treated was No. 303008. With no new stock on the horizon, a major refurbishment plan was instigated in 1984. The first unit to be overhauled was No. 303006. Eventually, fifty 303 units were refurbished at Glasgow Works, Springburn, all emerging in the new Strathclyde orange and black livery. During the upgrade in the works, the original forward view from behind the driver in the DTSO vehicles was lost, with a bulkhead wall erected. Many people considered the refurbishment a backward move, with the new 2+2 seating replacing the original 2+3. This reduced seating capacity from 236 to 160 in each unit. The overhaul also saw group standard headlights installed in place of the head code box and connecting gangways fitted within each unit.

The 311 units remained unrefurbished and were all withdrawn at the end of 1990 in various liveries following the introduction of Class 320 units onto the North Clyde services. However, Nos 311103 and 311104 were both converted for Sandite use. 303 units included in the refurbishment were Nos 303001/003/004/006/008–014/016/019–021/023/025/027–028/032–034/037–038/040/054/045–047/051/054–056/058/061/065/070–071/077/079–080/083/085/087/091. Due to the costs involved, three units managed to be repainted in Strathclyde orange but retained the original window frames. In conjunction with the refurbishment, BR Scottish Region declared that the new units would be driver-only operation (DOO). Finance had been made available to provide CCTV on platforms and also mirrors to assist the drivers. The NUR union called out strikes as guards would lose their jobs under what was termed the 'Strathclyde Manning Arrangements'. This was going to be applied all over most of Strathclyde. A number of strikes were organised, but, ultimately, progress won the day and any guards made redundant were accommodated into ticket examiner jobs and retained their old rate of pay. However, much disruption was caused.

In 1987, Hyndland Depot was short sightedly closed and all maintenance concentrated to Shields Depot. This was despite a wide campaign to keep it. The area once again was sold off for housing. In 1998, unit 049 had been transferred to Clacton Depot on the Eastern Region for departmental use. It was modified and took part in a jointly funded Network Rail South East/BR Research project to develop 'databus' technology. This unit was painted in full Network South East livery and renumbered 303999.

In 1992, development of the then 'Cross Rail' in London project had been based on a fleet of 140 four-car 341 units to operate between Reading/Aylesbury and Shenfield via central London to/from Colchester. It was planned that the fleet would feature an onboard control system using databus technology rather than a multi-wire control system. These trains would also feature on-board diagnostics, enabling faults to be identified and rectified. An automatic fault-logging system with land-based monitoring of the train equipment was envisaged plus there would be passenger information system. To test this feasibility of the equipment, databus was fitted to Blue Train No. 303049 and renumbered 303999. The databus was connected to an on-board radio, which transmitted and received data from line side equipment, feeding data to a control room and the units home depot. This unit was repainted into Network South East livery with test equipment supplied by Siemens and Plessey Controls. This consisted of hard wired on-train equipment, a cab-control system mounted in the middle of each cab and provision of new tightlock couplers between vehicles with an electrical drum connection passing data between vehicles. The equipment was used to test and develop the feasibility of driver-only operation (DOO) and the use of radio-based train to land communications. It was tested between November 1992 and December 1993. It was then returned to Shields Depot in Glasgow for component recovery before being scrapped in 1996.

After being used as Sandite units, No. 936104 was withdrawn and scrapped. However, No. 936103 was preserved at the Summerlee Heritage Centre Coatbridge, but one DTSO was later sold on for scrap. The refurbished 303 units remained in operation at the time of the UK privatisation with National Express, taking over the ScotRail franchise from 1998. Soon after unit Nos 303019/021/023/087 were repainted into Scottish Passenger Transport Executive (SPTE) carmine and cream livery. These were the only units painted in this livery. This was short-lived, as it was announced that with the new franchise a new order for new electric stock in the form of Class 334s was to take place. However, due to the delayed delivery of these units, a large number of the Class 303s were still active. By the millennium, the fleet was further reduced to thirty-six units. After the Class 334s finally entered service in 2001, it was the beginning of the end of the 303s, with eleven units eventually taken out of service by the end of the year. In much reduced numbers the others continued in traffic until 30 December 2002 when unit Nos 303011 and 303088 operated the last passenger service. The units were given a good send off with pipers and hundreds of enthusiasts and staff all along the north bank and at Helensburgh Central station. The units then worked empty to Yoker Yard. They, along with several others, soon made their way to Shields Depot for stripping and a few months later they were taken in batches to Immingham Furnace Smelter and recycled. One three-car 303 was preserved, being made of the DTSOs from unit No. 303032 and the MBSO of No. 303023.

The Blue Train nostalga was now established within ScotRail. The first unit, No. 303001, had been briefly returned to Caledonian Blue livery in 1985 to celebrate the 25th anniversary of their introduction following the withdrawal of the last unrefurbished units. ScotRail then took a much-praised decision to cobble together the best of the remaining coaches and return them to authentic 1960s look, with the exception of half-yellow warning panels. However, due to unit 001 being selected for refurbishment, No. 303048 then became the designated unit for preservation. Only the motor coach (MBSO 61824) was from the original unit. A voluntary group was then formed to help care for 048, which became a popular exhibit at BR open days during the early 1990s and was for a time successfully hired for charters and rail tours. Unfortunately, after a couple of years lying idle at Shields Depot in Glasgow, the unit was sent for scrap. The move angered enthusiasts, but Malcolm Reed, the then director general of the SPTE and chairman of the Scottish Branch of the Rail Heritage Committee, insisted that there was no alternative. He stated, 'I was party to that decision. Unfortunately the rules on asbestos are very strict. These days it is virtually impossible to preserve stock that contains blue asbestos.' However, as some readers may note, the three-car 126 DMU based at Bo'ness also had blue asbestos, which was removed by a specialist firm at Morecambe after a Lottery grant was given. After further discussions, the heritage committee decreed that a Blue Train should still be preserved as a monument to the modernisation of Scotland's railways, and as a result, the interior fittings of No. 303048 were removed and stored with the intention of returning the preserved unit based at Bo'ness back to its near original condition. In the end a combination of coaches from Nos 303023 and 303032 were saved.

Incidents and Accidents

Over the years the 303 and 311s have both been involved in many serious and fatal accidents, such as at Neilston, Paisley Gilmour Street and Pollokshields East. Unit 303051 was perhaps the unluckiest of all. Already notorious as the unit which exploded at Renton in 1960, it ran away during a shunting manoeuvre as it was being returned from Glasgow Works to Shields Depot following refurbishment in 1987. It collided head on with loco No. 37011 near Singer station and was subsequently scrapped without ever re-entering service. Another refurbished unit, No. 303038, spontaneously combusted in a siding within Shields Depot in 1991. The remaining units were subsequently rewired and given upgraded pantograph circulating oil. The elegant wrap-round front windows were another casualty replaced by smaller flat safety glass panel windows from 1972 after several drivers had been seriously injured or killed by vandalism. Unit No. 303091 was partially destroyed at Gower Street near Glasgow Central in August 1973 after striking the rear of Class 126 Diesel Power Car 51011. DTSOL 75857 was extensively damaged, but remarkably this coach was rebuilt and released back to traffic in 1977. The DMU coach was completely destroyed. Unit 091 was also one of the chosen units for refurbishment later in 1985.

Memories of the Class 303 and 311s

I travelled on the Class 303s and 311s regularly on the Argyle Line, Cathcart Circle, Newton and most other locations from 1965 until 2002. I attended college between 1978 and 1980 and earlier on numerous visits to my auntie's house at Croftfoot. They were excellent units to travel on and I was involved in very few failures. One unit I travelled on in September 1979 broke down at Croftfoot station. The unit had apparently a complete loss of power. I was on my way to college and before long another six-car 303 soon appeared, cautioned to the rear and shoved us into Glasgow Central as a nine car. I can't remember the unit numbers, but it was a Tuesday morning and the service was the 07.26 Newton to Glasgow Central. The distinctive sounds of the Class 303 are memorable, with the door-closing alarms, the compressor, the hiss of the air brakes, the sound of the handbrake being wound on, the sound in the motor coach when you passed over a neutral section overhead, the sounds of the motors, the ticking sound as the set accelerated and on arrival at a destination the escape of air. I always felt that the traction motors were miniature versions of the engines on the *Enterprise* in the original *Star Trek* series!

My last journey on a 303 was on Monday 30 December 2002 on board No. 303011 on the 09.27 Bellgrove to Helensburgh Central service, although I only travelled as far as Dalmuir to avoid the awaiting paparazzi at destination. I opted instead to video the six-car departing from Dalmuir. The 303 and 311s were generally well received by most train crews. Glasgow Central-based driver John Fisher recalled an incident in 1977. He had been driving a 311 unit from Wemyss Bay to Glasgow Central. On the approach to Hillington West, his unit ran over a shopping trolley placed on the line. As a result severe damage was caused, resulting in no power. The next service behind was a six-car Class 126 DMU ex-Ayr. After consultation with the control and with fitters on hand, the DMU was coupled up using the buck eyes from both units. However, no through electrical or braking was possible. Basically, the DMU pushed the three-car 311 to Glasgow Central at 20 mph. The fact that the bulk of the units lasted over forty years is testament to their great construction. As part of ScotRail's franchise commitment in 1998 (National Express), new more modern Class 334 Juniper units were built from 1999 to 2000 by Alstom in Birmingham to replace the last of the elderly 303/311 units. After an introduction plagued with teething problems, the Juniper fleet finally started to enter service in large numbers on the SPT network from 2001 to 2002, allowing the final Class 303 units to be withdrawn. Following withdrawal, most units were towed to Immingham Humberside for scrapping.

Depot Codes

ED – Eastfield Glasgow
GW – Shields Glasgow
HY – Hyndland Glasgow
HQ – Headquarters (BR)
LO – Longsight Manchester
PO – Private Owners

Route No. Codes and General 303 Information

Photos courtesy of Darrel Hendrie.

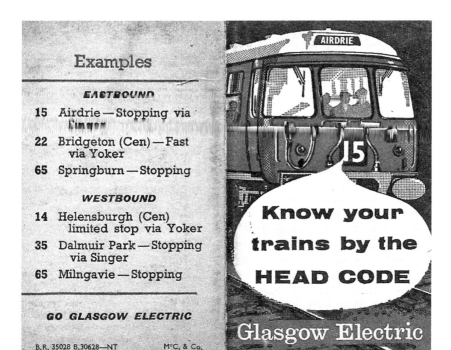

Examples

EASTBOUND

15 Airdrie — Stopping via Singer

22 Bridgeton (Cen) — Fast via Yoker

65 Springburn — Stopping

WESTBOUND

14 Helensburgh (Cen) limited stop via Yoker

35 Dalmuir Park — Stopping via Singer

65 Milngavie — Stopping

GO GLASGOW ELECTRIC

B.R. 35028 B.30628—NT   MᶜC. & Co.

AIRDRIE

Know your trains by the HEAD CODE

Glasgow Electric

 Glasgow Electric
HEAD CODE NUMBERS

Each GLASGOW ELECTRIC train displays a two-figure HEAD CODE at the front end.
It may help passengers to recognise their trains by knowing how the Head Code system works, and what the two numbers mean.

Left-hand number or letter indicates DESTINATION — thus

1	Helensburgh (Cen) or Airdrie
2	Balloch or Bridgeton (Cen)
3	Dalmuir Park
4	Clydebank (Cen)
5	Singer Works
6	Milngavie or Springburn
7	Partick Hill or Charing Cross
8	Craigendoran or Shettleston
9	Hyndland Depot
0	Queen Street
D	Dumbarton

Right-hand number indicates ROUTE and KIND OF TRAIN — thus

1	Fast via Singer *
2	Fast via Yoker
3	Limited Stop via Singer *
4	Limited Stop via Yoker
5	Stopping via Singer *
6	Stopping via Yoker
7	Workers
9	Empty

* Where no alternative routes exist, e.g. between Milngavie and Springburn, the number 1, 3 or 5 will always be used.

The Glasgow Blue Trains: 303 and 311 EMUs

The famous Blue Train portrait of a six-car 303 at Craigendoran Junction. This had been painted by the famous painter Terence Cuneo, who had been commissioned by British Railways. Note the cost of the article cover was 3s 6d – equal to approximately £5 in today's money. (December 1961; British Railways/C. Howat collection)

Interior shot of a DTS coach on a recently introduced Blue Train. (August 1962; British Railways/C. Howat collection)

View of a Blue Train motor brake second open coach under construction at the Pressed Steel
Factory in Linwood, near Paisley. (August 1959; British Railways/C. Howat collection)

Hyndland Depot – general view taken from one of the yard floodlights. The depot was a hive of
activity for many years, but BR decided to close it and concentrate maintenance to Shields Depot
from 1987. It was opened in 1961 to house the newly introduced Blue Train fleet. The depot
comprised nine roads, three of which were undercover and could house six units. It later became
home to the Class 314 fleet when introduced in 1979. (April 1960; Rodger Whip/Darrel Hendrie
collection)

No. 303035 (HY) at Hyndland Depot for maintenance. Note the plug doors facing outwards. This experiment was deemed unsuccessful, and the doors were later reconfigured to slide apart within their runners. (June 1966; Rodger Whip/Darrel Hendrie collection)

Driver Jim Morrison of Bridgeton Depot at the controls of a DT in unit No. 068. This unit was never refurbished. It was withdrawn in orange livery in January 1990 and scrapped later that year. (March 1979)

Nos 303086 and 311096 (Both GW) at platforms 3 and 4, Glasgow Central, with Hamilton Circle and Cathcart Circle services. 086 was scrapped in 1990 and 096 was stored from 1984 and scrapped at Wolverton England in 1989. (October 1979)

No. 303079 (GW) arrives at Hillington West station with a Gourock to Glasgow Central service. It was refurbished and withdrawn from traffic in 2000. (July 1979)

No. 303076 (HY) in mixed livery at High Street with a Milngavie to Springburn service. This unit remained unrefurbished and was withdrawn from traffic in September 1990 and scrapped in 1991. (July 1979)

No. 303048 (HY) departs Bridgeton Central with a Balloch via Singer service. Note the adjacent carriage sidings. On the reopening of the Argyle Line this station closed to passengers, but the sidings remained to carry out cleaning. This lasted until 1987 when all facilities were transferred to Yoker Yard. (October 1979)

No. 311109 (GW) arrives at platform 5 at Glasgow Central with a service from Neilston via Queens Park. This unit later received orange livery but was withdrawn in 1990. (July 1979)

No. 303051 (HY) arrives at Westerton with a Springburn to Milngavie service. This unit had an unlucky career. A transformer in the motor coach blew up at Renton in 1960. It was refurbished in 1987, but on its way from Glasgow Works back to Shields Depot was struck by a Class 37 so never worked in service and was scrapped in 1989. Note the symbol 'GG' below the window of the leading coach. This was for 'Greater Glasgow'. It was short-lived, but the forerunner of the SPT symbols to come. (July 1979)

Off the road – mishaps occasionally happen. No. 303074 (HY) became derailed at a set of catch points between Hyndland Depot and Partick. Rumour has it that a patient from the local hospital at Gartnavel had escaped and released the handbrakes! (May 1962; Darrel Hendrie collection)

No. 303040 (HY) in mixed livery due to borrowing a motor coach from another unit arrives at Port Glasgow with a Gourock to Glasgow Central service. It was refurbished and withdrawn in 2002. (July 1979)

Six-car 303 near High Street with a Helensburgh Central to Airdrie service. Note the Class 27 with brake van in the foreground. High Street Goods is to the right and the City Union lines to St Enoch and Shields Junction to the left. These have been proposed for a cross-city service on numerous occasions, but any proposals have never come to fruition. (November 1979)

Six-car 303 passes Parkhead Forge in the vicinity of Parkhead signal box with a westbound special from Airdrie to Hyndland Depot. Both units were involved on driver training duties. (July 1960; Ian McDonald/Darrel Hendrie collection)

Six-car 303 passes the recently closed Partickhill station with a Helensburgh Central to Argyle Street peak-hour service. This station was replaced by Partick, approximately 50 yards to the east, as part of the reopened Argyle Line. This was also to provide better connections with the underground system. (December 1979)

No. 303086 (GW) at Glasgow Central with a service to Kirkhill via Langside. Note the Class 45 loco behind the unit. This unit was refurbished but withdrawn from traffic in 1989. It was scrapped in 1990. (July 1979)

No. 303072 (GW) between Kings Park and Croftfoot with a Glasgow Central to Motherwell via Kirkhill and Blantyre service. This unit was not refurbished and was withdrawn from traffic in 1990 and scrapped the same year. (September 1979)

No. 303087 (GW) in mixed livery arrives at platform 13 at Glasgow Central with a service from Wemyss Bay. It was refurbished and was the last unit to retain wrap-round front windows, which did not disappear until 1977. It was given Strathclyde carmine and cream livery in 1998. It was withdrawn from traffic in 2001. (October 1979)

No. 311108 (GW) at Cathcart with an Inner Circle service to Glasgow Central. This unit was involved in a crash with a Class 116 DMU at Pollokshields East in 1974. It sustained minor damage and stayed in service until withdrawn in 1990 in blue and grey livery. (November 1979)

A three-car 311 comes off the Argyle Line and joins the West Coast Main Line at Rutherglen Central Junction. It was working a Dalmuir to Motherwell via Belshill service. Note the 'GG TransClyde' symbol on rear coach. (December 1980)

No. 303013 (HY) arrives at Hamilton West with a service from Glasgow Central via Belshill. These services were redeployed to run via the Glasgow Central Low Level on the reopening of the Argyle Line from November 1979. (July 1979)

Three-car 311 passes Glasgow Central signal box with a Wemyss Bay to Glasgow Central service. This box closed in 2012 and all panels were transferred to the West Of Scotland Signalling Centre at Springburn. (August 1980)

No. 303011 (GW) at the head of a six-car arrives at Kilwinning with a Largs to Glasgow Central service. The 303s had been utilised on this day due to a severe shortage of 318 units. (July 1990)

No. 303019 (HY), brand new having just been delivered to Hyndland Depot. This unit would receive many livery changes over the years and was in fact one of the few 303s to receive the Strathclyde carmine and cream livery in 1996. It was withdrawn from traffic in 2000. (May 1961; Rodger Whip/Darrel Hendrie collection)

Left: No. 303047 (HY) at Pollokshields East station with a Newton to Glasgow Central via Queens Park service. Note the unit still had the wrap-round windscreens. It was refurbished and was withdrawn in 2002. (August 1976)

Below: No. 303041 (GW) arrives at Maxwell Park station with a Glasgow Central to Cathcart Outer Circle service. This unit was not refurbished and was withdrawn from traffic in 1990. (April 1971; Bob Docherty)

Six-car 303, unit 023 (HY) leading arrives at platform 13 at Glasgow Central with a service from Gourock. This unit was refurbished and was later painted into carmine and cream Strathclyde Livery. It was withdrawn from traffic in 2002. (August 1979)

No. 311101 (HY) at Milngavie having just arrived on a service from Springburn. The platforms here were extended in 2021, but the branch still suffers from severe congestion due to the short-sighted singling of parts of the line in the early 1990s. (April 1986)

Above: No. 303056 (GW) passes Cathcart signal box with a Glasgow Central to Newton service. The unit is on the Cathcart station by pass line between Mount Florida and Kings Park stations. (April 1991; Darrel Hendrie)

Left: Six-car 303 in Lockerbie Loop, unit 006 (HY) leading. These units and others had been used for testing out the new overhead line equipment recently installed on the West Coast Main Line Electrification Project. (October 1973; Paul Strathdee/C. Howat collection)

A close up of the old wrap-round cab windows on unit No. 303041 (HY) arriving at Glasgow Central with a service from Gourock. Note the driver had already changed the destination blind for the next route, as was common at the time. (July 1976)

No. 303022 (HY) at Lanark with a limited stopping service to Milngavie. This unit crashed through the buffers at this station in 1975 but only suffered minor damage. It was stored in 1983 and scrapped in 1987. (August 1981)

No. 311110 (HY) at Balloch Central with a service to Airdrie via Singer. This unit was withdrawn and scrapped in August 1990. (May 1986)

Six-car 303, unit 071 (GW) leading arrives at Glasgow Central. This unit was refurbished but was involved in the Bellgrove crash in 1989. It was scrapped in 1990. (August 1979)

Six-car 303 and six-car 314 units both lie in the sidings north of Motherwell station. These sidings are still in use and are known as the 'Derby Sidings'. This was because from the 1960s onwards, Derby Class 107 and 116 DMU units were often stabled here. (April 1982)

No. 303039 (HY) arrives at Bellgrove with a Milngavie to Springburn via Singer service. This unit was not refurbished and was withdrawn and scrapped in 1990. (August 1981)

No. 311098 (GW) at Pollokshields West with a Glasgow Central to Cathcart Outer Circle service. This unit was withdrawn from traffic in August 1990. (April 1980)

No. 303039 (HY) arrives at Hyndland station with a Helensburgh Central to Airdrie limited stopping service. This unit was not refurbished and withdrawn and scrapped in 1990. (August 1981)

No. 311093 (GW) battles its way through the snow on the approach to Glasgow Central with a service from Kirkhill via Maxwell Park. (February 1986)

Six-car 303, unit 009 (HY) leading arrives at Dumbarton Central with a Springburn via Singer service. Unit 009 was refurbished and withdrawn in 2000. (August 1981)

Various withdrawn 303 and 311 units lying stabled in the former Bellahouston Sidings adjacent to Shields Depot Glasgow. Note the Mk 1 stock also on hand. These coaches would probably be used on the Glasgow Central to Carlisle via Kilmarnock services. Once again, due to short sightedness these sidings were sold off in the mid-1980s for a retail development and a golden opportunity for overspill sidings to help Shields Depot was missed. (August 1981)

No. 311107 (GW) has just come over the crossover at Kirkhill station to form a service to Glasgow Central via Langside. The driver has still to change the destination board. The local Kirkhill terminators were withdrawn in the late 1980s as part of a PTE review. The engineers moved in shortly after and removed another useful crossover. (August 1981)

Six-car 303 arrives at Garscadden with a Balloch Central to Bridgeton via Yoker service. Notice the old booking office and the electric sign on the overbridge. (October 1961; Bob Docherty)

No. 303058 (HY) arrives at Dalreoch with an Airdrie to Helensburgh Central via Singer service. This unit was refurbished and withdrawn in 2001. (August 1981)

No. 311093 (GW) at Muirend with a Neilston to Glasgow Central service. Muirend signal box was closed in 1980 and control was passed to Cathcart signal box. Unit 093 went into storage in 1984 and was scrapped in 1988. (May 1982)

No. 303052 arrives at Dalmuir with a Sunday Balloch Central to High Street via Yoker service. Unit 052 was not refurbished. It was the first unit to receive the new toughened front windscreens. It was withdrawn and scrapped in orange livery in 1990. (August 1981)

No. 303026 (HY) at Carstairs with an express peak-hour service to Anderston. This unit was not refurbished and scrapped in 1989. (August 1981)

No. 303070 (GW) approaches Glasgow Central with a service from Neilston. This unit was refurbished. It was withdrawn from traffic in 2001. (May 1980)

No. 303063 (HY) passes Hyndland signal box with a Helensburgh Central to Airdrie service. This unit was not refurbished and withdrawn from traffic in 1990. The signal box did not fare much better. It was demolished in 1987 and all work was transferred to Yoker Integrated Electronic Control Centre. (March 1980)

No. 311107 (GW) arrives in platform 7 at Glasgow Central with a service probably from Neilston. As was normal practice at the time, the driver has already changed the destination blind in anticipation of the return working. This unit was withdrawn and scrapped in 1990 in blue and grey livery. (August 1981)

No. 303021 (GW) at Kirkhill with a Newton to Glasgow Central via Queens Park service. This unit was refurbished and later painted in the Strathclyde carmine and cream livery. It was withdrawn from traffic in 2001. (February 1995)

Nos 311093 (HY) and 303046 (HY) at Helensburgh Central. Both were booked to work services to Airdrie. Unit 093 on an express and 046 behind with a stopping service all stations via Yoker. 093 was stored in 1984 and scrapped in 1988. 046 was refurbished but was later involved in the Wemyss Bay accident in 1994 caused by vandals. (April 1986)

No. 311108 (HY) at Glasgow Central Low Level with a Motherwell to Dalmuir via Singer service. This unit was involved in a fatal crash at Pollokshields East in June 1974 when it collided with a Class 116 three-car DMU on an East Kilbride service. Slight damage occurred but it was quickly returned to traffic. It was withdrawn from traffic in August 1990. (May 1986)

No. 303055 (HY) arrives at Barnhill station with a Balloch Pier to Springburn via Singer service. It was refurbished and retained its original window fittings. It was also the last unit to retain the original Caledonian blue livery until 1969. (June 1981)

No. 311094 (GW) at Mount Florida with a Glasgow Central to Newton via Kirkhill service. This unit was withdrawn in 1988 and scrapped in 1990. (April 1980)

Six-car 303, unit 023 (GW) leading on the Dubbs to Byrehill spur south of Kilwinning with a shuttle special between Ardrossan Harbour and Ayr. This was in connection with an open day at Ayr Townhead. This unit was later painted in the Strathclyde carmine and cream livery. (June 1989)

No. 303028 (HY) arrives at Bearsden with an Airdrie service. It was refurbished but withdrawn from traffic in May 1999, donating its motor coach to unit 037. The line from Westerton Junction to Milngavie was singled in parts by overzealous engineers in the early 1990s despite objections from the public. Due to these restrictions, any late running is now extremely difficult to recover from. (August 1981)

Two six-car 303 units awaiting their next turns of duty at Helensburgh Central station. Note on the extreme left is platform 4. This was removed in the late 1980s. (August 1981)

No. 311101 (HY) at Springburn with a Milngavie-bound service. This unit with No. 303007 was involved in a crash with a cement train at Rutherglen in 1975. Both were slightly damaged and repaired. It was withdrawn from service and scrapped in August 1990. (April 1986)

Nos 311104 and 311105 (Both HY) at Airdrie station and sidings. The sidings were reduced from four to one in the early 1990s to facilitate a larger car park. Unit 104 went on to become a Sandite unit. 105 was withdrawn from traffic and scrapped in 1990. (April 1986)

No. 311103 (GW) inside Glasgow Works receiving an overhaul. This was the last unit to remain with all yellow ends. It was withdrawn from passenger traffic in August 1990 but got a new lease of life as a Sandite unit along with No. 311104. It was finally withdrawn from traffic in 1996. It was saved from the scrap man and obtained by the Summerlee Heritage Trust near Coatbridge and survives boarded up but minus one of the DT coaches. (June 1981)

No. 303086 (GW) departs Glasgow Central with a service to Gourock. This unit was refurbished but withdrawn in 1989. It was scrapped in 1990. (May 1980)

Elizabeth II arrives at Argyle Street station to officially reopen the Argyle Line through Glasgow Central Low Level. The official date was 1 November 1979. She travelled on a brand-new 314 unit to Partick. This line was closed between December 1994 and December 1995 after severe flooding caused substantial damage. During this closure, Motherwell to Dalmuir services were diverted to Glasgow Central High Level and Lanark to Milngavie services were diverted via Whifflet and Queen Street Low Level. (November 1979)

No. 303049 (HY) at Rutherglen station with a Motherwell to Dumbarton Central via Singer service. This unit was transferred to the Midland Region as surplus in 1981. It was later sent to the Eastern Region to Clacton Depot and became a Sandite and later a test unit. It was renumbered 303999. It was eventually sent back to Glasgow and scrapped at Shields Depot in 1996. (January 1980)

Left: No. 303016 (HY) crosses the Clyde west of Dalmarnock with a Milngavie to Lanark express. This unit was refurbished and withdrawn from traffic in 2001. (January 1980)

Below: No. 303035 (HY) at Glasgow Central Low Level with a Dalmuir to Motherwell service. This unit was unique for two reasons. Firstly, it was temporarily fitted with external plug doors and later fitted with thryristor control equipment. This control offered better energy consumption, reduced maintenance, smoother acceleration and various other advantages. However, it was not adopted. This unit was not refurbished and was scrapped in 1982. (March 1980)

A Class 303 departs from the recently re-sited Rutherglen station and heads onto the Argyle Line with a westbound service. The Class 20 with the brake van hovering in the foreground is on the Rutherglen West Curve awaiting access to Bridgeton Yard. (September 1980)

No. 303042 (HY) arrives at Argyle Street with a Dalmuir to Motherwell service. This unit was unrefurbished and withdrawn and scrapped in 1990. However, certain coaches were later donated to the reformed unit 048 in Caledonian blue livery. (March 1980)

Six-car 303 with unit 009 leading (GW) approaches Cathcart signal box with a Newton to Glasgow Central via Queens Park service. The unit is between Cathcart East and North Junction. This unit was refurbished and withdrawn in 2000. The signal box closed in 2015 when control transferred to the WSCC at Springburn. (April 1991; Darrel Hendrie)

DT 75590 of unit 303025 (GW) lying in the Sidings at Yoker Depot. The unit was destroyed by the usual act of mindless vandalism and was later taken to Shields Depot. It was stripped for spares before being taken to MC Metals at Glasgow Works. (November 2001; Darrel Hendrie)

Above: Six-car 303, unit 037 (GW) leading resting between duties at Airdrie. This line was extended as a single track to Drumgelloch in 1989. In 2010 it was reopened all the way to Bathgate as a double line and provides a comprehensive service between Airdrie and Edinburgh. (August 1981)

Right: No. 303039 (HY) emerges out of Stobcross Tunnel towards Glasgow Central with a Motherwell to Dalmuir via Yoker service. This unit was not refurbished and withdrawn and scrapped in 1990. (March 1980)

Three-car 303 approaches Springburn station with a service from Balloch Central. The unit is passing the former Sighthill East Junction signal box. This box closed in 1992 and all work was transferred to Cowlairs Signalling Centre. In 2013 this control was further transferred to Edinburgh Signalling Centre. (June 1981)

Interior view from behind the driver on a 303 unit near Wishaw on a Carstairs to Anderston morning peak service. On the opposite direction a six-car 303/311 combination heads south to Lanark with a service from Milngavie. (August 1981)

No. 303009 (HY) arrives at Motherwell with a Dumbarton Central via Blantyre and Singer service. This unit was refurbished and was withdrawn from traffic in 2001. (March 1980)

No. 303013 (HY) emerges out of Glasgow Queen Street Low Level station with a Balloch Central to High Street limited stopping service. This unit was refurbished and withdrawn from traffic in 2001. (August 1981)

No. 303027 (HY) stabled in the sidings at Carlisle. This unit was on hand to give London Midland drivers training for the forthcoming exodus of Blue Train units from Hyndland and Shields Depots to Crewe and Manchester. It later returned to Shields Depot and was refurbished. It was withdrawn in 2001. (August 1981)

No. 311096 (GW) at Bishopton with a Wemyss Bay to Glasgow Central service. Note, just at the end of the platform, the crossover to the MOD factory which is now long gone. Unit 096 was stored in 1984 and scrapped at Wolverton England. (August 1981)

No. 311095 (GW) approaches Mount Florida station with a Neilston to Glasgow Central service. This unit was scrapped in 1989. (August 1981)

Six-car 303, unit 063 (GW) leading arrives at Newton station with a Dalmuir to Motherwell via Belshill service. Unit 063 was not refurbished and was withdrawn from traffic in 1990. (May 1983)

No. 311100 (GW) comes off the Balloch Branch and arrives at Dalreoch with a Balloch Central to Bridgeton Central via Yoker service. This unit went into storage in 1983 and was scrapped in 1987. (October 1978; Rodger Whip/Darrel Hendrie collection)

No. 311097 (GW) arrives at Woodhall with a Glasgow Central to Wemyss Bay service. This unit was not refurbished and withdrawn from traffic in 1989. (August 1981)

No. 303026 (HY) at Airdrie with a service to Balloch Central via Singer. This unit was scrapped in 1989. (April 1984)

No. 303028 (GW) outside Glasgow Central in the 'Jungle' with two classmates. This unit was refurbished and withdrawn in 1999. Its motor coach was donated to unit 037. (October 1997)

Above: No. 311092 (GW) at Gourock ready to depart with a service back to Glasgow Central. This unit was not refurbished and withdrawn in 1989. (June 1984)

Left: Six-car 303, unit 043 (HY) leading arrives at Dalmuir with an Airdrie to Helensburgh Central via Singer service. Unit 043 was refurbished and was withdrawn in 2002. (August 1981)

No. 303081 (GW) arrives at Greenock Central with a Glasgow Central to Gourock service. This unit was withdrawn with asbestos problems in 1988 and scrapped in 1990. (May 1983)

No. 303046 (HY) bypasses Newton station with a Carstairs to Anderston limited stopping service. This unit was refurbished but withdrawn from traffic in 1994 after sustaining accident damage caused by vandals. (May 1982)

No. 303083 (GW) at Croftfoot with a football supporters special from Lanark to Kings Park. This unit was refurbished and withdrawn from service in 2001. (May 1982)

Three-car 303 approaches Hamilton West with a Dalmuir to Motherwell via Blantyre service. Note the sidings on the left. These belonged to Hamilton Diesel Depot, which dealt with mainly 105, 107 and 116 DMU units. This depot closed in June 1982. (April 1982)

No. 311100 (GW) at Wallneuk Junction just north of Paisley Gilmour Street on the slow lines with a Wemyss Bay to Glasgow Central service. The unit would be bypassed at Arkleston Junction by a DMU from Ayr. This unit went into storage in 1983 and was scrapped in 1987. (May 1982)

No. 303012 (GW) at Motherwell with a Dalmuir to Coatbridge Central service. This unit was the first unit to receive the blue and grey Clyderail livery. It was refurbished and withdrawn in 2002. (May 2001)

No. 303080 (GW) arrives at Neilston High with ECS from the nearby Uplawmoor Sidings. This station was renamed Neilston in 1985. The SPTE had planned to truncate this station in the mid-1980s with services terminating/starting from Whitecraigs. Fortunately, this never happened, but it is bizarre that the line was never electrified the short distance to Uplawmoor or even Lugton. (August 1981)

The relaunch of No. 303048 (GW) at Shields Depot along with piper. The unit went on to provide further service with ScotRail and was involved in many specials. It was originally intended to preserve this unit, but due to asbestos contamination it was eventually scrapped in 1996. (May 1991; Bob Docherty)

No. 311099 (GW) departs Glasgow Central with a Newton via Maxwell Park service. This unit was not refurbished and withdrawn from traffic in 1990. (May 1984)

No. 303027 (HY) passes Muirhouse North Junction with a Kirkhill to Glasgow Central via Langside service. This unit was refurbished and lasted until 2002. The relay room to the right was a former signal box and was in use until 1974, when its operation was transferred to Glasgow Central Signalling Centre. (July 1976)

No. 303070 (GW) at Wemyss Bay having arrived with a service from Glasgow Central. This unit was refurbished and was the first unit to be fitted with through gangways in 1985. It was withdrawn in 2001. (August 1981)

Six-car 303, unit 006 (HY) leading arrives at Drumchapel with an Airdrie to Helensburgh Central via Singer service. Unit 006 was the first unit to be life extended under the refurbishment agreement and was withdrawn in 2001. (August 1981)

No. 311108 (GW) arrives at Port Glasgow with a Glasgow Central to Gourock service. This unit was involved in a fatal crash at Pollokshields East in June 1974 when it collided with a Class 116 three-car DMU on an East Kilbride service. Slight damage occurred but it was quickly returned to service. It was withdrawn from traffic in August 1990. (July 1981)

Old meets the new at Gourock station. No. 303028 (GW) having recently arrived on a service from Glasgow in platform 1 is beside a brand-new six-car 318, unit 255 (GW) trailing. The new breed of 318s were on driver training. (June 1986)

No. 303023 (HY) with DMU unit 101328 (ED) at Springburn. This was in the days when passengers from Glasgow Queen Street Low Level had to change at Springburn for the onward connection to Cumbernauld. Nowadays services simply reverse at Springburn with services usually started from Dumbarton Central or Dalmuir. A proposal was made in the 1990s to insert a spur just north of Bellgrove at Haghill Junction with a tunnel to allow direct access onto the Cumbernauld line to avoid the reversing moves, but this has never been pursued by Transport Scotland. (May 1986)

No. 303091 (GW) at Neilston with a service to Glasgow Central. This was the unit involved in the crash at Gower Street near Shields Junction south of Glasgow Central in August 1973. It collided into the rear of a Swindon six-car 126 DMU resulting in DMU Power Car No. SC 51011 sustaining substantial damage and being withdrawn from traffic. Unit 091 was remarkably rebuilt and back in service from 1977 and was also refurbished in 1987. It was withdrawn in 2001. (May 1986)

Three-car refurbished 303 takes the Argyle Line at Kelvinhaugh Junction with a Dalmuir to Motherwell service. The lines behind the unit continue to Charing Cross and Queen Street Low Level on the North Electric system. (April 1989)

No. 303024 (GW) departs from Paisley Gilmour Street with a Wemyss Bay to Glasgow Central service. This unit was refurbished and withdrawn in 2001. (May 1988)

Nine-car 303, unit 047 (GW) leading in the east sidings at Corkerhill Depot. The M77 was later built behind the trees making any chance of expansion slim. (April 1989)

No. 311109 (GW) at Pollokshaws East with a Glasgow Central to Cathcart Inner Circle service. This unit later received orange livery but was withdrawn in 1990. (April 1980)

Six-car 303, unit 023 (GW) leading at Ardrossan Harbour with a shuttle special to Ayr. This was in connection with an open day at Ayr Townhead Depot. This unit was later painted in the Strathclyde carmine and cream livery. (June 1989)

Six-car 303 passes Polmadie Depot with a diverted Motherwell to Glasgow Central service. The diversion was due to the Argyle Line being closed reaction to flooding. 303s also occasionally visited this depot in the 1980s for washing only. (April 1995)

No. 303041 (HQ) in Greater Manchester livery parked outside Shields Depot in Glasgow. It had been returned from the LMR for asset stripping. It was officially withdrawn in 1990. (May 1988)

No. 303081 (HQ) lying withdrawn at Falkland Yard in Ayr with a 101 DMU for company. Many withdrawn units were stabled around the Ayr and Kilmarnock areas prior to onward movement to the blast furnaces at Immingham in Humberside. (March 1988)

No. 303089 (GW) at Clydebank with a service from Motherwell to Dalmuir. This unit was refurbished. It was the last unit to carry a headcode in service in September 1978. It was also named *Cowal Highland Gathering 1884–1994*. It was withdrawn in 2001. (June 1990)

No. 303043 (GW) departs Partick with a Dalmuir to Motherwell via Blantyre service. This unit was withdrawn at the end of 2002. (October 2002)

No. 303014 (GW) at Helensburgh Central with ECS to Yoker Yard. This unit was refurbished. It was withdrawn from traffic in 2002. (September 1991)

No. 303089 (GW) at Croftfoot with a diverted Glasgow Central to Motherwell via Blantyre service. Low level services were suspended long term due to the Argyle Line being closed reaction to flooding and also due to engineering work around the Polmadie area. (January 1995)

No. 303999 (HQ) stabled at Shields Depot prior to being scrapped. Originally No. 303049, it was transferred to the LMR region in 1981 and worked around the Manchester area. It was then moved to the Eastern region to Clacton and became a Sandite unit and later on also converted into a test train. It was finally scrapped in 1996. (March 1995)

No. 303048 (HQ) at Shields Depot Glasgow. This unit was transferred to the LMR region in 1983 and worked around the Manchester area. It was withdrawn from service in 1990 and transferred back to Shields Depot. It was repainted into Caledonian blue livery and was earmarked for preservation. However asbestos-related problems dashed this and it was scrapped. (March 1995)

No. 303056 (GW) takes the Clydesdale Lines with a diverted Glasgow Central to Motherwell service. The main line had been closed at Eglinton Street due to engineering works. (March 1995)

Nos 303037 and 303047 (Both GW) in the sidings at Corkerhill Depot prior to afternoon departures. Driver Michael Magna of the same depot gave me a hurl on unit 047 ECS into Glasgow Central. (August 1986)

No. 303086 (GW) at Glasgow Central platform 1 with a diverted service to Motherwell via Kings Park and Blantyre. All services were unable to run direct to Motherwell due to engineering operations between Eglinton Street and Polmadie. (March 1995)

No. 303090 (GW) just south of Mount Florida station with a Glasgow Central to Newton service. This unit was refurbished. It was withdrawn from traffic in 2001. (May 1980)

No. 936104 (GW) at Kilwinning. This was the former No. 311104. It had been converted for Sandite use in 1990. It was used until 1996 when Network Rail replaced it and sister No. 936103 with more modern sanding machines. (March 1996)

Six-car 303, unit 011 (GW) leading south of Irvine near Gailes with a golf special from Glasgow Central to Troon. The special was bringing golf fans to Troon for the Open Golf. (July 1997)

No. 303065 (GW) arrives at Lanark station with a service from Dalmuir via Yoker. This unit was refurbished and withdrawn in 2002. (August 1997)

No. 303087 (GW) outside Glasgow Central with a Cathcart Outer Circle service. This unit was refurbished in 1986 and given the Strathclyde carmine and cream livery in 1998. It was withdrawn in 2001. (May 1999)

Left: No. 303022 (HY) approaches Drumchapel with a Sunday Helensburgh Central to Airdrie via Singer service. This unit was withdrawn from traffic in 1987. (August 1981)

Below: No. 303047 (GW) approaches Hyndland station with a Dalmuir to Coatbride Central via Singer and Blantyre service. This unit was refurbished in 1987 and withdrawn in 2002. (June 2001)

No. 303033 (GW) departs from Glasgow Queen Street Low Level and heads into the gloom of the Queen Street Tunnel towards High Street on a Helensburgh Central to Airdrie service. (May 1998)

No. 303040 (HY) in mixed livery due to borrowing a motor coach arrives at Glasgow Central with a Gourock to Glasgow Central service. This unit was refurbished and withdrawn in 2002. (August 1979)

No. 303020 (GW) arrives at Whifflet with a Dalmuir to Coatbridge Central service. This unit was refurbished in 1986 and withdrawn in 2002. Note the lines to the left. Although double, they become single and connect the south side electric system with the north near Coatbridge at Sunnyside Junction. They were used extensively in 1995 during the period the Argyle Line was closed due to flooding and still acts as an emergency route if the Argyle Line is closed for any other reasons. This allows maintenance units an alternative route from Yoker Yard to Shields Depot. (May 2000)

No. 303048 (GW) approaches Craigendoran Junction with a working from Airdrie to Helensburgh Central. (May 1994; Bob Docherty)

No. 311110 (HY) at Dumbarton Central with a Helensburgh Central to Airdrie via Singer service. This unit was withdrawn and scrapped in 1990. (May 1986)

No. 303051 (GW) at Hyndland Depot Sidings after the infamous collision with No. 37011 near Singer. The unit had just been refurbished at great cost, but higher authority decided that it was still not worth fixing it again. (March 1987; Bill Gracie/C. Howat collection)

Left: No. 303021 (GW) at Glasgow Central with a service for Gourock. This unit was refurbished and given the Strathclyde carmine and cream livery in 1998. It was finally withdrawn from traffic in 2002. (May 2001)

Below: No. 303008 (GW) with No. 318250 (GW) at the buffers of platforms 10 and 11 at Glasgow Central. Unit 008 had just arrived on a service from Gourock. The 318 was about to depart with a service back to Gourock. Unit 008 was the first to be refurbished with the Strathclyde orange and black livery. It was withdrawn in 2001. (May 1999)

No. 303047 (GW) arrives at Paisley Gilmour Street with a Glasgow Central to Gourock service. This unit was refurbished and lasted until 2001. (September 1986)

No. 303041 (LO) at the buffers at Manchester Piccadilly station alongside a couple of Class 142 diesel units. This unit was withdrawn from traffic in 1990. (August 1987)

No. 303006 (GW) at Kilwinning platform 2. The unit had been on a test run from Shields Depot. The driver was about to change ends and take the unit back to the depot for further checks. It was refurbished and withdrawn in 2002. (May 2000)

A Class 311 passes the site of Kelvinhaugh signal box with a Springburn to Milngavie service. The main building in the background was the old Yorkhill Hospital for sick children. The signal box had been closed in November 1979, on the opening of the Argyle Line, when Hyndland Box took over. Kevinhaugh signal box was demolished shortly after. (February 1980)

Right: No. 303022 (HY) departs from Glasgow Central with a service to Hamilton Central via Blantyre. This unit crashed through the buffers at Lanark in July 1975 but only sustained minor damage. It was taken into storage from May 1983 and finally scrapped in 1987. (July 1976)

Below: No. 303090 (GW) at Paisley Gilmour Street with a Gourock to Glasgow Central service. This service stopped at all stations after Paisley. This unit was refurbished in 1987 and withdrawn in 2002. (June 1984)

No. 303048 (GW) is seen at platform 11 at Glasgow Central with a 150th anniversary special to Gourock. This was the celebration of the Glasgow to Paisley Gilmour Street and Gourock Railway. The unit was for VIPs and this was the first run of the refurbished unit after repairs at Shields Depot. (March 1991; Darrel Hendrie)

No. 303011 (HY) emerges out of Dalmarnock Tunnel into the new Bridgeton Argyle Line station with a Motherwell to Dumbarton Central via Singer service. This unit was refurbished and was involved in the very last Blue Train run with unit 088 in December 2002. (May 1983)

No. 303063 (HY) at Motherwell with a Milngavie to Lanark limited stopping service. This unit was not refurbished and was withdrawn from traffic in October 1990. (May 1986)

No. 303089 (GW) at the buffers of platform No 6 Glasgow Central with a Neilston via Queens Park service. This unit was the last to carry the old two figure headcode numbers in service. It was also named *Cowal Highland Gathering 1884–1994* in August 1994 at Gourock. It was withdrawn from traffic in 2001. (July 1995)

Two 303s at Queens Park station. On the left, unit 090 (GW) heading a Glasgow Central to Newton service, and on the right, an unidentified cousin arrives on a Neilston to Glasgow Central service. (May 1980)

A three-car 311 passes Cathcart signal box with a Neilston to Glasgow Central service. Cathcart signal box finally closed in 2015 and a new panel opened up and replaced it in the West Of Scotland Signalling Centre at Springburn on the north side of Glasgow. (May 1980)

Corkerhill Depot: A general view after the morning peak of Class 303s and a 156 Sprinter unit. The depot was electrified in 1984. However, it is now working beyond capacity and is struggling for space similar to Shields Depot. (May 1988)

No. 303085 (GW) at Croftfoot with a Kirkhill to Glasgow Central via Langside service. This unit was refurbished and lasted until 2001. (May 1980)

No. 303025 (GW) approaching Glasgow Central with a service from Newton via Queens Park. The unit was destroyed by a fire caused by vandalism at Yoker Yard in August 2001. It was later taken to Shields Depot and stripped for spares before being taken to MC Metals at Glasgow Works. (February 1999)

No. 303016 (HY) at Charing Cross with a Helensburgh Central to Airdrie service. This unit was refurbished. It was withdrawn from traffic in 2001. (April 1980)

No. 303064 (HY) at Finnieston with a Lanark to Milngavie limited stopping service. This station was renamed Exhibition Centre in 1986. This unit was not refurbished. It was withdrawn from traffic in 1988 and cannibalised. It was eventually scrapped in 1990. (May 1980)

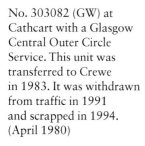

No. 303082 (GW) at Cathcart with a Glasgow Central Outer Circle Service. This unit was transferred to Crewe in 1983. It was withdrawn from traffic in 1991 and scrapped in 1994. (April 1980)

No. 303081 (GW) at Platform No 4 Gourock stabled between duties. This unit was withdrawn with asbestos problems in 1988 and scrapped by 1990. (May 1984)

No. 303075 (GW) with a couple of 318 units inside Shields Depot Glasgow. The unit was getting a regular maintenance check. (September 1986)

No. 303087 (GW) arrives at Glasgow Central with a Cathcart Inner Circle service. This unit was refurbished. It was the last unit to retain wrap round front windows which did not disappear until 1977. It was given Strathclyde carmine and cream livery 1998 and withdrawn from traffic in 2001. (May 1980)

No. 303004 (HY) at Dalmuir with a Milngavie to Lanark limited stopping service. This unit was refurbished. It was withdrawn from traffic in 2000. (April 1980)

No. 303085 (GW) at Crosshill with a Newton to Glasgow Central via Queens Park service. This unit was refurbished. It was withdrawn from traffic in 2001. (April 1980)

No. 303015 (HY) at Bellgrove with a Helensburgh Central to Airdrie service. This unit was withdrawn with asbestos problems in 1987 and scrapped in 1988. (September 1986)

Six-car 303, 037 (HY) leading at Alexandria Parade with a Balloch Central to Springburn service. This unit was refurbished but was unfortunately involved in the Newton crash in 1991 with 314203 (GW). However, it was repaired and remained in traffic until 1999. (May 1980)

No. 303064 (HY) at Motherwell with a Carstairs to Partick limited stopping peak-hour service. This unit was withdrawn from traffic in 1988 and scrapped in 1990. (May 1986)

No. 303046 (HY) passes Dumbarton Central signal box with an Airdrie to Helensburgh Central service. This unit was refurbished but was withdrawn from traffic in 1994 after being badly damaged by vandals near Wemyss Bay. (May 1986)

No. 303048 (GW) at Ayr Depot. The unit was on display as part of an open day. This depot closed in 2010. This unit was originally earmarked for preservation but due to asbestos issues never made it and was replaced by other vehicles. It was transferred to Leith in 1981, withdrawn in 1991 and transferred back to Shields Depot Glasgow where it was repainted. It was scrapped minus the fittings in 1998. (June 1991)

No. 303046 (GW) approaches Glasgow Central with a service from Newton via Langside. This unit was withdrawn from traffic in 1994 after the Wemyss Bay accident. (June 1991)

No. 303041 (LO) at Manchester Piccadilly with a service to Altrincham. This unit was transferred to Manchester in 1981 and withdrawn from traffic in February 1990. (August 1987)

Six-car 303, unit 077 (GW) leading at Saltcoats. Between 1996 and 2000 a six-car 303 was rostered in the evening peak between Glasgow Central and Ardrossan Town as not enough 318s could be diagrammed. This gave a welcome break to commuters, although no toilets were available. (May 1999)

Six-car 303 at Drumchapel, unit 062 (HY) trailing working a Helensburgh Central to Airdrie via Yoker service. Unit 062 was not refurbished and withdrawn and scrapped in 1990. (August 1981)

No. 303091 (GW) arrives at Newton with a service from Glasgow Central via Maxwell Park. This unit was involved in the crash at Gower Street near Ibrox in August 1973 with Swindon Class 126 Power Car No. SC 51011. It sustained substantial damage but the damaged DT coach was remarkably rebuilt and back in service from 1977 and was refurbished in 1987. It was withdrawn in 2001. (May 1986)

No. 311109 (GW) and a
Class 101 DMU race towards
Paisley Gilmour Street.
Unit 109 was on a service
from Gourock. The DMU was
on a service from Ardrossan
Winton Pier. Unit 109
received orange livery but
was withdrawn from traffic
in 1990. It seems strange over
the years that no one has ever
thought of putting a single
line connection from the Up
Ayr to the Down Gourock.
(May 1983)

No. 303032 (HY) at
platform 5, Dalmuir. It had
just arrived with a service
from Motherwell and was
awaiting the signal to proceed
ECS to Yoker Depot. This
unit was refurbished and both
driving trailers made it into
preservation. (May 1986)

No. 311107 (GW) approaches
Dumbarton Central with
a Helensburgh Central to
Airdrie via Singer service.
This unit was withdrawn and
scrapped in 1990 in blue and
grey livery. (February 1990;
Darrel Hendrie)

No. 303053 (LO) at
Manchester Piccadilly with
a service to Macclesfield.
This unit was transferred
to Manchester in 1983
and withdrawn from
traffic January 1990.
(August 1987)

No. 303048 (GW) at
Prestwick International
Airport with a special from
Glasgow Central. This visit
was in connection with
the opening of the station
and had just dropped off
VIPs. The unit then ran to
Ayr station and later took
the VIPs back to Glasgow
Central. (September 1994;
Darrel Hendrie)

Six-car 303, unit 003 (GW)
leading arrives at Newton
station with a Dalmuir to
Motherwell via Blantyre
service. Unit 003 was
refurbished and lasted
until 2000. (June 1996)

No. 311104 (GW) stabled at Edinburgh Waverley. The unit was stabled in between driver training duties. Nos 311103 and 303048 were also used. Eventually it was decided to use Class 305 units from England on the Edinburgh to North Berwick services. (March 1990; Darrel Hendrie collection)

No. 303004 (GW) at Partick station with a Dalmuir to Motherwell via Blantyre service. This unit was refurbished and withdrawn from traffic at the end of 2002. (October 2002)

Nos 311105 and 311108 (Both HQ) stored at Ayr Depot. Both were awaiting onward transit to the breakers yard at Immingham Humberside. Ayr Depot closed its doors in 2010 when DB Cargo pulled out and the depot was completely demolished from January 2019. (November 1990)

Old meets new again. This time at the old platform 13 at Glasgow Central. Due to the protracted arrival of the Class 334s, the 303s got an extra couple of years on our railway. (May 2000)

The 303 interior as we liked to remember them. This was a shot taken inside the BDT of NO. 303048 at Ayr Depot. (June 1991; Darrel Hendrie)

The end is near. Units 303087, 045 and DT 75590 lie at Yoker Depot awaiting their moves to the scrap merchants. (November 2001; Darrel Hendrie)

End of the line. The cut-up remains of unit 303005 (HQ) at MC Metals Glasgow Works. (June 1991; Darrel Hendrie)

Preserved Nos 303032/023 (PO) combined coaches in the shed at the SRPS shed at Bo'ness. The preserved unit was made up of the DT coaches of unit 032 and the motor coach of unit 023. They have been pushed and pulled up the branch to Manuel on numerous occasions. (June 2014)

No. 311103 (PO) stabled in sidings at the Summerlee Heritage Centre near Coatbridge. Unfortunately, one of the driving trailers was sold for scrap. However, there is another 303 DT from No. 303013 in use as an anti-terrorism trainer with the Metropolitan Police at Gravesend. (June 2022; James Fraser)